SHIPS-IN-BOTTLES

Written and Illustrated by
Donald Hubbard

SHIPS-IN-BOTTLES

A STEP-BY-STEP GUIDE TO A VENERABLE NAUTICAL CRAFT

David & Charles: Newton Abbot

ISBN 0 7153 5491 4

First published in Great Britain by David & Charles (Publishers) Limited, 1971

Designed by Joan O'Connor

*To my father, Ernest F.
Hubbard, whose curiosity
and interest in everything
inspired me to attempt to build
my first ship-in-a-bottle*

CONTENTS

SHIPS-IN-BOTTLES

ACKNOWLEDGMENTS

Even a slim volume such as this could not be produced without the inspiration, cooperation, and assistance of others. My own indebtedness extends to many people: including Dr. and Mrs. Steve Bernocco, who set me on the trail of ship-in-bottle art while we served together in Guantanamo Bay, Cuba, and who possess the first model I constructed; to my wife, Darlene, for her thoughtful suggestions and careful editing of the manuscript; and to Bill Hemming and Jim Steinbaugh, my business partners, who carried my share of the workload while I pondered line drawings, sentence structure, and photographs.

I am deeply grateful to Dr. G. Burton Appleford of San Diego, California, who generously permitted me to use his collection of ship-in-bottle reference material to insure my complete coverage of the literature about this little-known art; and to Mr. George D. Wintress, Assistant Vice President of The Seamen's Bank for Savings in the City of New York, for permitting us to examine the bank's fine collection of nautical art and to photograph certain notable examples for this book.

I must offer my most sincere thanks to Walton Rawls of McGraw-Hill for his months of friendly correspondence and for his organizational and editorial guidance as we waded through the problems of putting this book in final form.

Finally, I wish to express my appreciation to all those incredulous people who provided me with supreme and often welcome amusement by exclaiming, "You're writing a book about WHAT?"

D.H.

Coronado, California
March 1971

INTRODUCTION

The technique of putting ships into bottles developed during the early years of the 19th century in the forecastles of the old sailing ships. In an era when sea voyages lasted months and years, and entertainment was self-evolved, off-watch sailormen occupied themselves creating bits of nautical folk art from whatever raw material came to hand. On whaling vessels the most abundant scrap materials were the teeth and bones of whales and walruses, which the whalermen fabricated into the many familiar items collectively known as scrimshaw. But other materials such as wood and rope and yarn were also used, and many interesting and decorative objects were made from these. It is not surprising then that an empty bottle might have piqued the imagination of some long-gone salt and led him to devise the technique for displaying miniature ships we describe in this book.

Whatever the origin, the technique for putting ships into bottles was well known to sailormen of all the major seafaring nations. Evidence of their work can be found in nautical museums throughout Europe and on both coasts of the United States. The collection in The Seamen's Bank for Savings in the City of New York includes approximately 100 examples housed in bottles ranging from gallon size down to miniatures smaller than a hen's egg. Good examples can also be found in nautical collections in Europe such as the Nationaal Scheepvaartmuseum in Antwerp, Belgium; Museo Maritimo in Barcelona, Spain; The Glasgow Art Gallery and Museum in Scotland; the Musée de Saint Malo, Chateau de St. Malo, France; the Sandefjord Sjøfartsmuseum in Sandefjord, Norway, and the National Maritime Museum, Greenwich, England.

Unfortunately, despite widespread knowledge of the technique, good early examples of ship-in-bottle art have become scarce. Even well-known dealers in maritime art rarely have them available, and when they do chance upon one the price quoted is well outside what most individuals would be willing to pay. This is a shame, for there are few decorations as evocatively nautical as a ship-in-a-bottle. Even crude examples foster vivid memories of the sea, and a model which has been carefully done can stand by itself as a true work of art.

For the individual who wishes to possess a ship in a bottle, there is no question that the least expensive and most interesting way to obtain one is to make it. With the materials available to the hobbyist today it is possible for even a beginner to create a truly beautiful model. And with experience there is no limit to the type or style of sailing vessel one can build.

If you don't already know, the secret of these small vessels is that they are built outside the bottle in complete detail, but with folding masts and movable spars. The ship is then inserted into the bottle with the masts down and with the spars turned parallel to the axis of the hull. Once the ship is inside, and in place, fore-and-aft lines (extensions of the stays, which run from the masts, through the bowsprit, and out the mouth of the bottle) are pulled to erect the masts. The other spars are then carefully positioned via a long wand through the bottle's mouth to give an authentic appearance, and the bottle is sealed.

There is nothing difficult about the process beyond the necessity to operate on a rather small scale. However, even this can be compensated for by mounting a magnifying glass on a stand and by working slowly. Certainly there is no requirement for delicate fingers and hands, or no jack-tar "forebitter" could ever have assembled one.

Here is an authentic maritime hobby to which you need only devote a reasonable amount of time, but one which will greatly reward you with the satisfaction of creating and owning a small reminder of the great age of sail.

NAUTICAL TERMINOLOGY

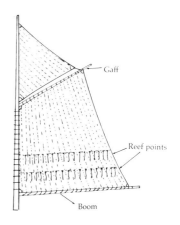

Boom; Gaff; Reef Points

Since it is necessary to use nautical names for things throughout this book it seems sensible to place this glossary at the very beginning. If you are an old nautical hand you can skip this section; however, if your knowledge of ships and rigging is sketchy you might find a short review of the terminology helpful.

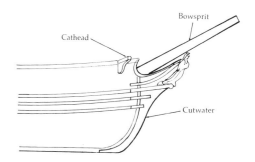

Bowsprit; Cutwater Cathead

Abeam	On a line at right angles to a ship's keel.
Aft	At, in, or toward the stern of a ship.
Bitt	A deck post around which ropes or cables are wound and held fast.
Boom	A spar along the bottom edge or foot of a fore-and-aft sail.
Bow	The forward end of a ship.
Bowsprit	A large spar projecting forward from the bow of a ship.
Braces	On a square-rigged ship a rope by which the yard is swung about and secured horizontally.

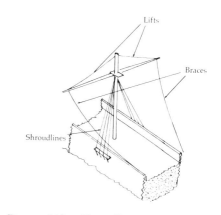

Braces; Lifts; Shroudlines

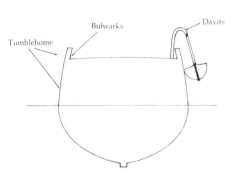

Bulwarks; Davits; Tumblehome

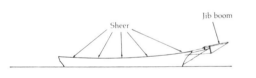

Jib boom; Sheer

Bulwarks	The sides of a ship that project above the upper decks.
Cathead	A projecting beam located near the bow of a vessel to which the anchor is hoisted.
Cutwater	A strengthening timber bolted to the forward portion of a vessel's stem as protection and often for decoration.
Davits	Devices projecting over the side or stern of a ship used for hoisting and lowering small boats.
Forebitt	One of the bitts near the foremast.
Forebitter	Nautical slang for an old salt often found relaxing against a forebitt busily at work on some handicraft.
Forecastle	The part of a ship in front of the foremast, where the sailors' quarters are.
Gaff	A spar along the upper edge of a fore-and-aft sail.
Gunwales	The upper edge of the sides of a ship or boat.
Jib boom	A spar forming a continuation of the bowsprit (In this book bowsprit includes the jib boom).
Lifts	On a square-rigged ship a rope used to support and vertically adjust the yards.
Mast	A substantial vertical spar used to support the sails and other spars.

Port	The left side of a ship when one faces forward.
Reef points	Short pieces of line attached to a sail for use in reefing (gathering up the base of a sail to reduce its area).
Sheer	The fore-and-aft curvature of a ship's deck as seen in a side view.
Shroudlines	The ropes which provide lateral support to a ship's mast.
Spar	Any of the stout poles used in a ship's rigging, such as masts, booms, gaffs, and yards.
Stanchions	Posts which support the rails around exposed decks.
Starboard	The right side of a ship when one faces forward.
Stays	Ropes used to support a mast in a fore-and-aft direction.
Staysail	Any sail which is supported by a stay.
Stem	The entire forward edge of the bow.
Stern	The after part of a ship.
Tumblehome	The inward curve of a ship's hull above the waterline designed to increase stability or improve water flow when heeled over.
Yards	Crosswise spars used to support square sails.

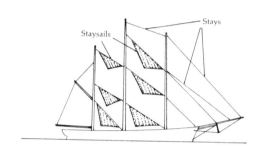

Stays; Staysails

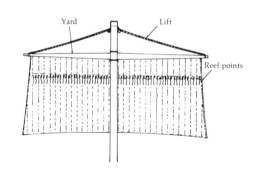

Yard; Lift; Reef Points

TOOLS AND MATERIAL

You probably have many of the items listed below among your household and hobby supplies. What you are missing can be obtained easily at the local hardware, hobby, or variety store. The other things can be made by you in a few minutes. You may even think of substitutes that will serve as well or better than the materials listed.

Basic Materials Needed

Clear glass bottle (see Chapter 3).
Half-pint can of linseed oil putty (see Chapter 3).
Block of wood for the hull, 3 x 1¼ x ¾ inches (see Chapter 4).
Two feet of ¹⁄₁₆ inch diameter birch doweling, or a package of thin (⅛ inch or less) bamboo cocktail skewers (see Chapter 6).
Spool of No. 60 black nylon or silk thread.
Spool of No. 30 gauge galvanized wire.
Small bottle of clear nail polish.
Small bottle of white glue.
Several sheets of sandpaper—grades 120, 150, 200.
Small paintbrush, some thinner, and model enamel in white, black, and other colors as desired.
Selection of artists' oil colors—Prussian Blue, Titanium White, and Viridian if desired (see Chapter 3).

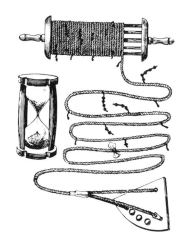

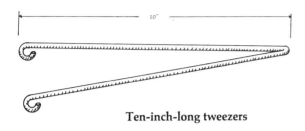

Ten-inch-long tweezers

Small ball of ⅛ inch diameter cotton fishing line.
Stick of red sealing wax.
Several sheets of medium weight bond paper.

Tools to Get

Exacto knife or single-edge razor blade for carving the hull and other general uses.
Electric drill for turning masts and spars to size.
Pin vise and small drill bits (sizes No. 75 and 60) for drilling fine holes in hull and spars.
Soldering iron.
Tin snips.
Small screwdriver.
Fine-toothed saw or hacksaw blade.
Small vise.

Tools to Make

Fabricate the following tools from pieces of wire coat hanger and small pieces of metal cut from a tin can:

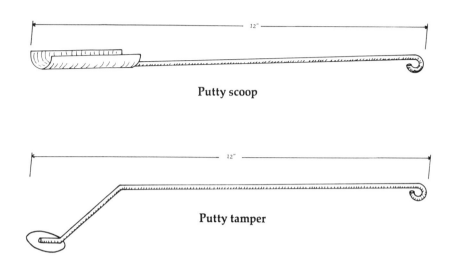

Putty scoop

Putty tamper

Ten-inch-long tweezers. This instrument will enable you to insert the ship into the bottle with reasonable control. Cover the tips with masking tape to prevent scratching your small ship.

Putty scoop. This will be used to put the "sea" into the bottle. To make this, cut a piece of metal about 2½ x ¾ inches out of a common tin can. Bend this to fit through the neck of your bottle and solder on a 12 inch handle fashioned from coat hanger wire.

Putty tamper. You will use this tool to level out your putty "sea" and to form the waves. Cut a small disk the size of a dime from a tin can and solder a coat-hanger-wire handle to it. This handle will have to be bent so that you can easily reach all areas of the bottle.

Positioning wire. You will need this to adjust the position of the ship and its sails once it is in the bottle. You will also have other uses for this general tool, such as touching white paint to wave tops, wake, and bow waves. Bend a ¾ to 1 inch angle at one end of a 12-inch-long piece of coat hanger wire.

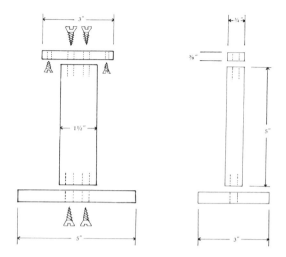

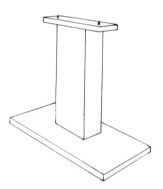

Plan for the workstand

Workstand

Finally, construct a small workstand out of scrap wood using the plan provided. The stand serves the dual purposes of providing a solid eye-level platform for working and it keeps the model from getting entangled in the clutter of your worktable. To avoid splitting your hull, be sure to use very narrow gauge screws where you anchor your ship to the stand.

SELECTING A MODEL
TO BUILD

Before you begin, it is best to decide which type of ship model you wish to build. A host of factors could influence this decision, ranging from the sentimental (Grandpa sailed on a square-rigger) to the availability of a good set of plans or a suitable illustration. From the standpoint of a beginner, possibly the most crucial factors will be availability of plans and complexity of the rigging.

Through the centuries, countless different types of ships and rigging evolved to meet changing conditions and purposes. Some of the best-known of these are illustrated in the silhouettes shown on these pages. Generally speaking, ships with square sails like barks and brigantines present more of a problem to the model builder than those with a fore-and-aft rig like the gaff schooners. The same rationale applies to the number of masts, the more there are the more difficult the overall problem becomes. The beginning builder should note that the degree of difficulty estimated does not apply just to the problems encountered in building the model. More complex riggings also require somewhat more care and skill when it comes time to insert the model into the bottle and cement it in place.

Sloop

Ketch

Three-masted coastal schooner

Gaff-rigged schooner

In this book we have chosen to make a model of a Gloucester Fishing Schooner to illustrate the steps in building a ship-in-a-bottle. This vessel calls for all of the basic steps involved in constructing other miniature ships and is so uncluttered in design that each step can be clearly shown. This model is well within the capabilities of even the beginning craftsman to execute and makes an interesting decoration whether perfect or not. Additionally, of course, it takes less time to build and therefore permits the beginner to proceed from step to step more rapidly. From a learning standpoint this is important, but it is also important to the person who has only a limited time to spend on a hobby.

Barque

Brigantine

Once you have decided upon the type of model you wish to construct, you must then concern yourself with its dimensions so that you can select a suitable bottle. To some extent both decisions are interrelated. That is, you may already have a suitable bottle on hand you wish to use. In this case your choice of model type may have to be determined on that basis, or you may have to alter the scale of the model you have chosen so that it will fit. In this book we have scaled our plans for the model to fit a short square bottle of standard size. If you wish to build the model of the Gloucester Schooner your selection of a bottle should approximate the dimensions which are outlined in the following section.

Square-rigger

Plan for Gloucester Schooner

Scale 1:1

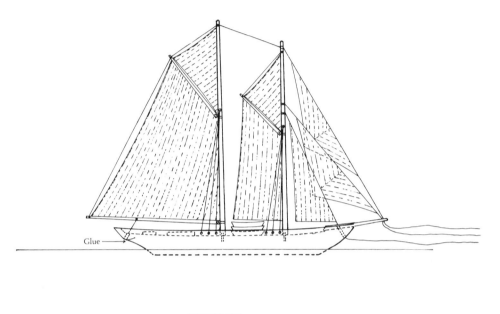

Glue

History—Gloucester Schooner—Because of its location near the Grand Banks, Gloucester, Massachusetts, became an important fishing port during the mid-1800s. Her fleet fished the stormy off-shore waters, and when the holds were full the schooners raced back to port to obtain the best prices for their catch. To meet the demands of its calling the Gloucester Schooner evolved as a tough, fast, seaworthy little vessel. A portrait of the *Bluenose*, a Canadian vessel of this same type, now graces the Canadian ten cent piece, and the *L. A. Dutton*, built in 1920, can be seen in Mystic Seaport, Connecticut.

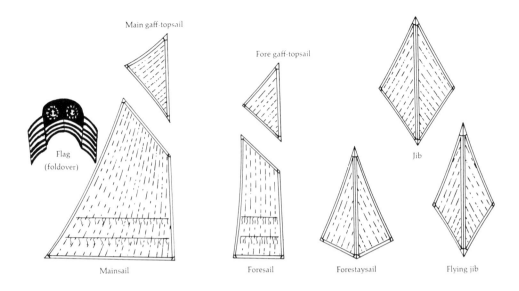

Main gaff-topsail

Fore gaff-topsail

Flag
(foldover)

Mainsail

Foresail

Forestaysail

Jib

Flying jib

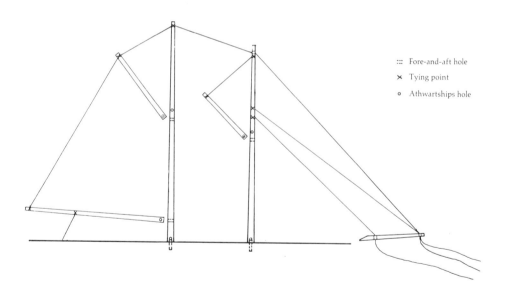

∷ Fore-and-aft hole

✗ Tying point

○ Athwartships hole

Color scheme—Dark green hull, white trim on rails, masts, and spar tips. White dories. Dark brown deckhouses.

SELECTING AND PREPARING THE BOTTLE

Selecting the right bottle for your ship model should be an early decision since it takes anywhere from two to four weeks for the putty "sea" to harden once you have prepared it. In choosing a suitable bottle, you should consider that its size and shape have a bearing on the ultimate appearance of your model. Ships of three or more masts look best in long slender bottles, while small coastal schooners and fishing vessels of one or two masts rest more comfortably in shorter bottles.

The bottle you settle on must have enough room inside for the sea, the ship's hull, and the erected masts. All of the plans in this book require a bottle with an outside diameter of approximately 3½ inches and a neck opening of ⅝ to ¾ inches. A bottle with these dimensions should not be too difficult to find since they seem to be reasonably standard.

From the standpoint of ease of display, a bottle with flat sides automatically eliminates the problem of rolling.

Pilot schooner

However, round bottles can be stabilized with a minimum of fuss by a few lumps of sealing wax melted to form a base.

Don't worry about minor distortions in the glass, for these are natural enough and do not present a problem. In fact, they seem to bring a bit of life to the ship as it is viewed from different angles. The seam (a small raised line on the glass formed where the two halves of the mold meet) is another problem you can't avoid. Just be certain to position the bottle so that the seam is not in the field of view (usually straight up and down) and it won't be noticed.

Baltimore schooner

For the serious hobbyist who is striving for authenticity in appearance the selection of a good hand-blown bottle might be worthwhile. Look for these in antique shops and be certain that they meet your requirements in neck diameter and clarity. Hand-blown bottles are not inexpensive, but they do add an old-time flavor which can more than offset their cost. Some of the less elaborate Christmas gift bottles are good choices, and they often offer the advantage of an extra wide mouth. Examination of the wares of the local liquor store should widen the list of possible choices and perhaps add a few pleasurable minutes to your search.

Mixing oil paint and putty

Once you have selected your bottle, you will have to rinse it well and thoroughly dry the inside before you are ready to insert the putty "sea." If your local tap water has a high chemical content, drying spots may appear on the inside of the glass. These are easy to remove by rubbing them with a piece of paper towel or Kleenex wrapped around a coat hanger wire.

Next, you must prepare your "sea." Open your can of putty and pour off half the linseed oil which you find floating on top. This will hasten the drying of the putty and keep it more manageable. Mix the remaining putty

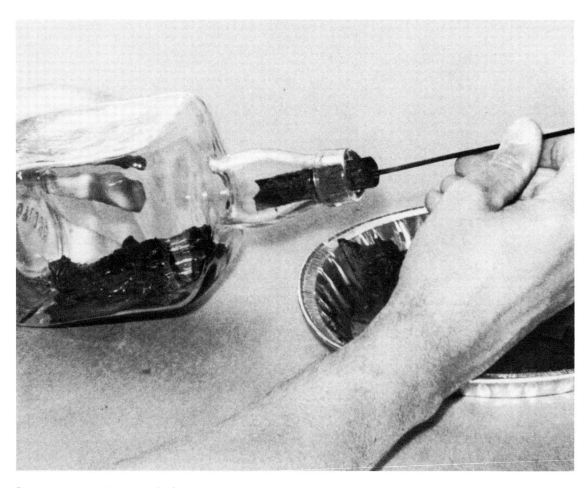

Inserting putty "sea" into the bottle

and oil with Prussian Blue artists' oil color. If the model you have selected is of the coastal variety, add sufficient Viridian to impart the slightly greenish tinge characteristic of near-shore waters. (Nutrients from the land permit the growth of tiny planktonic animal and plant life which imparts the coloration. Further offshore the nutrients are not usually as common, and the sea is a deep blue.) Whatever you do, make the sea good and dark. Light blue or light green seas are unnatural looking and don't provide sufficient contrast for convincing white caps or bow waves.

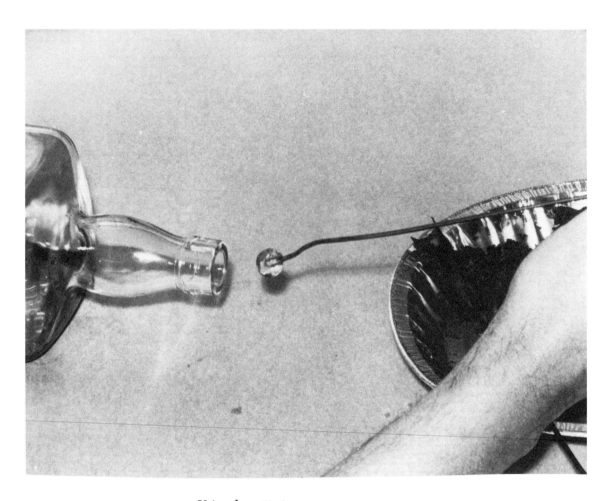

Using the putty tamper

Use your homemade putty scoop or a similar device to slide the colored putty into the bottle in small amounts. Be careful to avoid touching the sides of the bottle with putty, or you will leave oil stains on the glass which have to be removed later on. However, don't wait too long, for linseed oil tends to harden into a stiff, sticky mess. Removing it later requires some type of thinner to do an effective job. Keep the bottle level. If you don't, the soft putty will shift inside and leave thin, blue "high water" marks.

Aim for about ¼ inch depth of putty in the bottle, or, if you chose something short and "dimpled" like a "Pinch" bottle, use ¼ inch under the model and slightly more in the surrounding area to make the sea level. This will leave plenty of depth for pushing out waves and helps give a feeling of solidity to your model. On the other hand, too much putty should be avoided for several reasons. Thick applications take too long to harden and often tend to crack as they do. The putty also adds weight and reduces the height of the area in which the masts must fit.

Once you think you have enough putty inside, take your putty tamper and spread the mixture out evenly. This may require bending the wire handle to reach the inside shoulders of the bottle.

Prepare a bed for your ship by flattening an area in the center of the putty about ½ x 3 inches. Sink the bed down a fraction of an inch into the mass of putty. Push up a bow wave and roughly indicate some waves out to the sides of the ship caused by its movement. Remember, a ship displaces water as it moves.

Now consider how your sails are to be set. Keep in mind that most of the waves in the sea are caused by the wind, not the motion of the ship. These waves should be coming from the direction of the wind, and the wind should be blowing against the side of the ship, not directly at the bow.

The sea on most decent sailing days presents individual wave crests with white caps rather than long, even rolling swells. This helps you out. Gouge here and there and push up wave crests. You won't be in any great danger of messing up the job. If you make an obvious mistake, just push the putty back and have another try. Later, after the "sea" is dry, your touching up the wave crests with white paint will add immensely to their natural appearance.

Once you have your putty inserted and the seas shaped to your satisfaction, check the inside of the bottle for oil smudges. Again, remove these with a piece of pa-

Painting on the white caps with a piece of bent wire

per towel or Kleenex wrapped around a wire. Check your work by viewing the bottle against a light.

Now place your bottle on a level surface with the mouth open to allow the putty to set. The length of time required for drying will depend on the amount of linseed oil left in the putty when it was mixed, and on the air circulation in your chosen location. When the surface of the putty is no longer tacky the job is complete.

Now you can add white caps and bow waves. The "L" shaped wire tool is excellent for this. Open a tube of white artists' oil color, pick up a bit of the paint on the tip of the wire, and dab it onto the tops of the waves. Unlike a paintbrush the wire hops around a bit, but this helps to give your bursting seas a slightly wilder and natural look.

Don't forget to whiten the bow wave, and lightly indicate the boiling wake of your ship. The area behind a moving vessel is not a solid mass of white water but more of a churning mixture of subdued white and blue-green.

Keep the ship's bed free of paint, if possible, to insure a good bond when you finally cement the ship in place.

There is no real need to wait for the oil paint to dry prior to inserting your ship in the bottle, provided that you work carefully. Just be certain that you keep the ship's hull and sails out of the wet paint.

A selection of notable examples of the art

SHAPING THE HULL

The wood you select for the hull should be close-grained and blemish-free. It also should be reasonably easy to carve, sand, and drill without splitting. Balsa wood is too soft and splits too easily, while some of the harder woods, like oak, are too difficult to work. I normally use clear white fir, which meets all of my requirements and is easy to find. There are many other possibilities, and any similar wood such as white pine or spruce will work just as well.

Your job will proceed much more smoothly if you use sharp tools. Dull blades will not cut finely and tend to split the wood. Replacement blades for hobby knives are generally easy to obtain, and razor blades are always available. Discard the old blades promptly when they no longer cut properly and replace them.

Basic hull pattern for the Gloucester fishing schooner

Line indicating the desired curve of the deck

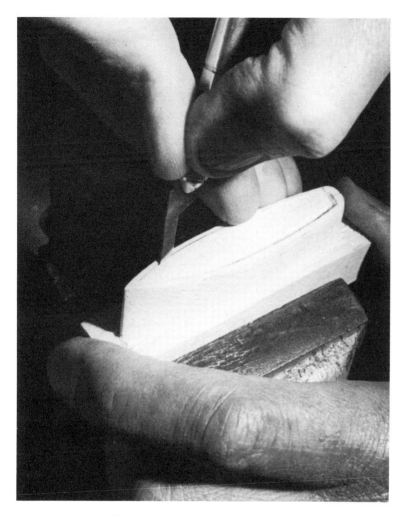

Begin with a piece of wood about 3 x 1¼ x ¾ inches. Place it in a vise narrow side up and trace out your deck outline. Cut or saw directly down from this outline to a ¾ inch depth to give yourself plenty of wood to work with.

Next, mark the sheer (curve) of the deck on the side of the roughed-out hull and cut away the excess wood. Sand the deck smooth, using a piece of fine sandpaper on a square block.

Finish carving your deck by lightly marking off the raised portions and bulwarks and then by removing the excess wood with a small chisel (Exacto blade No. 17

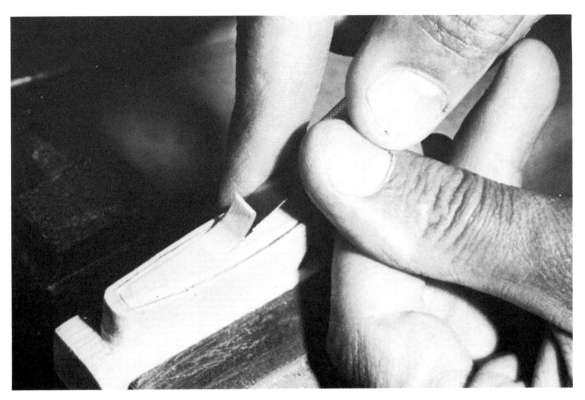

Chiseling out excess wood to form the deck

works well here). When completed, the bulwarks should be about $\frac{1}{16}$ inch thick as well as deep. Smooth the newly cut-out area with a small piece of folded sandpaper.

The most difficult part of carving the hull is behind you. Finish forming your bow and stern by trimming away the excess wood and by sanding the curves and by sharpening the stem.

Mark the waterline and carefully saw the hull from the block. Smooth out any irregularities and fasten the finished hull to your workstand with one of the small, narrow gauge screws provided.

Give the entire hull a coating of clear nail polish to seal it. I recommend nail polish rather than varnish since it comes in a handy container, is easily available, imparts a fine glossy coating, and also serves as an effective cement in other circumstances. Next give the portions of the hull to be painted two coats of colored enamel. Leave

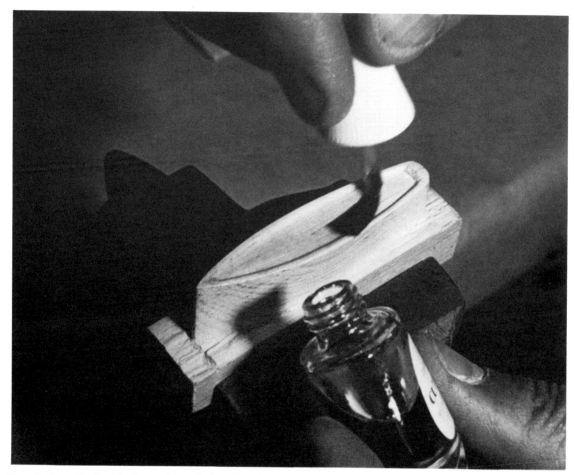

The deck and bulwarks formed, sanded, and receiving a coat of clear polish

Shaping the bow and stern

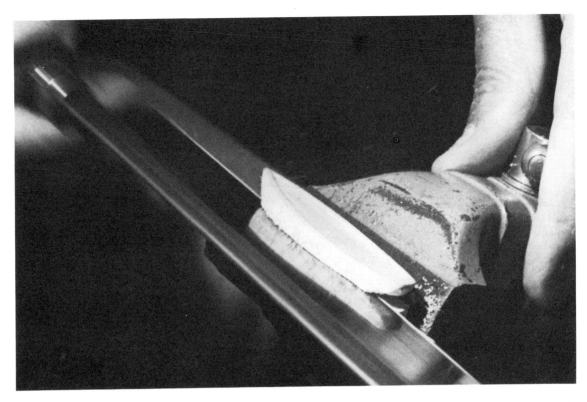

Sawing the completed hull from the block

the deck itself unpainted except for the clear nail polish coating.

If you wish to add some raised lines or strakes along the length of your hull to delineate the tops and bottoms of gun ports, or for decorative purposes, the easiest and surest way to do this is to use thread. Paint will not work well since it is almost impossible to paint consistently thick straight lines on models of this small scale.

To mark your gun ports, glue on two parallel lines of black thread approximately 2 millimeters apart and positioned roughly midway between the waterline and the bulwarks. With this accomplished the individual ports can be painted in using white enamel and a fine brush.

Decorative markings are easily added in the same way by using a single line of white or bright yellow thread glued along the hull just below the edge of the deck.

THE DECK

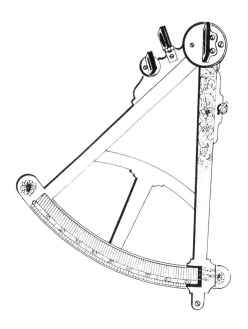

Very little has to be done to the deck of your model after the final carving and sanding of the hull are completed. However, depending on how much detail you wish, a touch of authenticity may be gained by adding small items such as hatch covers, deckhouses, lifeboats, and rails.

Popsicle sticks and tongue depressors make good material for deckhouses and hatch covers. They are readily sawed into small squares and split easily if too thick for your purpose. Sand them lightly and paint them dark brown to contrast with the unpainted decks. A touch of clear nail polish will cement them in place.

Carve your lifeboats from the same material as the hull. It helps to shape these very tiny boats while still attached to the end of a piece of wood; after sanding and painting them, cut them free and cement them in place.

Rails are easily made from No. 30 wire. Using your No. 75 drill bit, bore holes along the deck edge where

Making deckhouses from popsicle sticks

stanchions are to be located and insert short pieces of up-right wire. (It is easy to cut all of your stanchions to the proper length at the same time if you lay twenty or thirty pieces of wire across a strip of masking tape and cut the tape lengthwise with scissors.) Level the tops of all the inserted wires, coat them with clear nail polish, and while they are drying bend and shape a longer piece of wire to form the rail. Cement this to the tops of the stanchions with clear polish and paint.

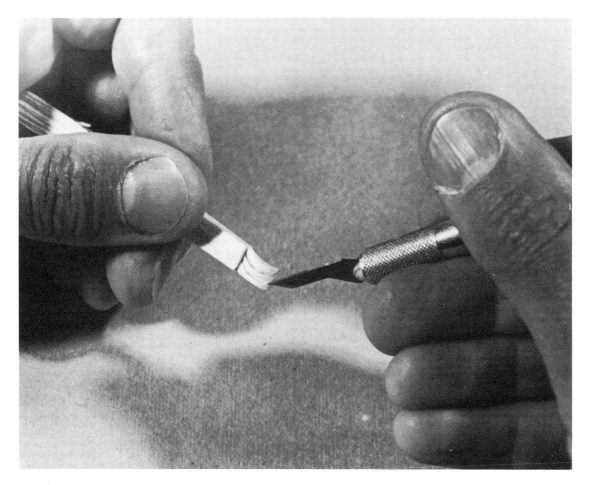

Carving stacked dories from the end of a piece of wood

If you find that working with wire is too difficult, you can form your guard rails with thread. Rails formed in this manner will not appear as finely made, but they are an acceptable substitute nonetheless.

Fasten your thread at the top of each stanchion with a tight clove hitch, beginning at one side and working around to the other. Be certain, as you proceed, that the thread does not sag between stanchions and that all the knots are evenly aligned. Finish the work at each end by

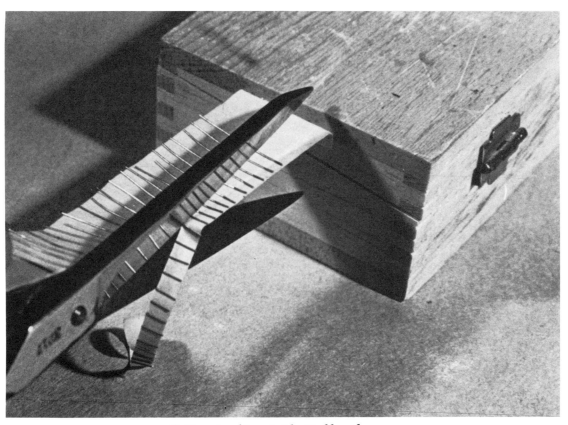

Cutting stanchions to identical length

carrying a length of thread down to the lower bulwarks and cementing it in place. Give the entire rail a coating of clear nail polish as a stiffener before final painting.

Lifeboat davits are made and mounted in the same way as the stanchions.

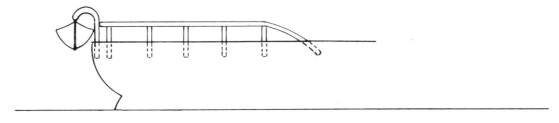

Rails, stanchions, and lifeboat davits

THE SPARS AND RIGGING

Generally speaking the job you do on the spars and rigging will be the most telling factor in the final appearance of your small ship. You had an opportunity to look at a variety of ship rigs in the section which deals with the selection of a model to build. If you return to that section you will note that every line has a purpose and ends at a logical place. If the model you are building is one of your own design, be certain to study carefully the illustration from which it was derived. If you have never before paid attention to a ship's rigging, it will pay you to seek out photographs or drawings of many ships and study them for a few minutes. Nothing in their rigging is there by accident, and because of this the entire maze of lifts, braces, sheets, shrouds, and stays presents a certain symmetry which gives each ship a beauty of its own. Let one line be out of place and even an untrained eye will spot it. The same applies to your model. You might as well forget about inventing your own rigging and sail plans; these have been worked out and established over a long stretch of time. It is up to you to copy your illustration or plan as closely as possible if you wish to produce an authentic looking job.

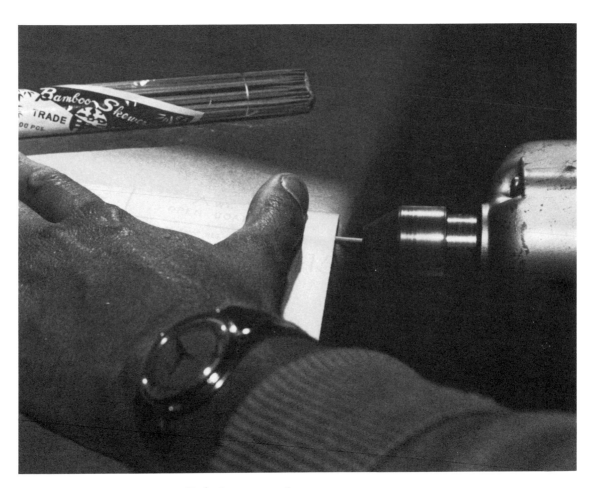

Reducing spars to size

Before you begin, you should be aware of the following points:

1. For an authentic appearance your spars should be less than $\frac{1}{16}$ inch in diameter. However, this is not difficult to achieve if you use an electric drill and turn your material to size between two pieces of sandpaper. Some hobby shops can supply birch doweling in $\frac{1}{16}$ inch diameter, which you can easily reduce to any size by the above method. If birch doweling is not available, try using thin bamboo cocktail skewers which are sold in packages of

Filing a needle section into a drill

about 100 in most variety stores. These have a slight tendency to split, but work out well if you take your time. Should all else fail, cut strips from straight-grained tongue depressors and sand round.

2. After turning your material to size, give it a coat of clear nail polish. This imparts a good gloss finish and helps prevent splitting when the wood is being drilled.

3. When drilling holes in the spars let the drill do the work. Don't apply too much downward pressure or you may split the wood. Incidentally, if you can't locate a fine drill point like the No. 75, try breaking a needle in half and filing the point flat on three sides. This is what the old-timers did, and it works.

4. If you do accidentally split the spar while drilling, try salvaging the job by tightly tying a small clove hitch around the split with thread and then coat it with nail polish. Trim the loose ends of the thread after the polish dries. As a matter of fact, all knots should be given a coat of polish before trimming to keep them tight.

5. Pushing No. 60 thread through the tiny drilled holes is reasonably simple if you coat the end of the

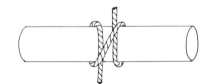

Clove hitch

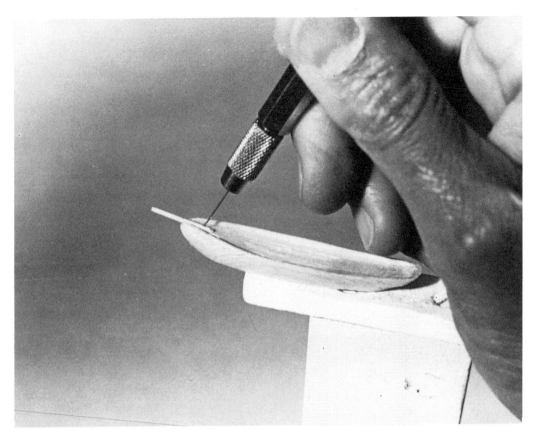

Drilling the bowsprit holes

thread with nail polish. This will stiffen the thread end and also prevent unraveling.

The first spar you attach is your bowsprit (actually bowsprit and jib boom), which is glued to your hull. There are two ways to do this. If you wish you may glue the bowsprit directly to the foredeck, but flatten the section that will be in contact with the foredeck to provide as much gluing surface as possible. Coat both surfaces (the deck and bowsprit) with nail polish and press together. For insurance run another coat of polish over the top of the joined pair and let dry. As an alternative you can sink the base of your bowsprit into the hull. Drill a hole with your No. 60 drill at the point where foredeck

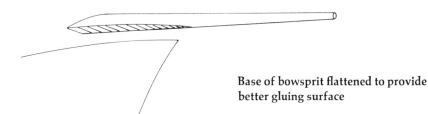

Base of bowsprit flattened to provide better gluing surface

and bow meet. Apply a good coat of clear polish to the bowsprit, slide it into the drilled hole, and let dry. Make sure the hole is sufficiently deep to provide a solid base. Regardless of which technique you use, keep in mind that the bowsprit will be subject to lifting pressure when you pull the threads to erect the mast, so it must be solidly attached to the hull.

Once the bowsprit has been firmly attached to the hull, you can mark it and drill the holes indicated on the plans.

The masts and their spars are next. Masts should be slightly thicker than the other spars and will look more authentic if they taper toward the top. Consult your plans and cut the masts to the proper length, then mark and drill the holes indicated. Note that some of the holes should be drilled to accommodate lines running fore-and-aft and others are for lines running through from side to side.

Do one mast at a time. Cut, drill, and attach the various yards, booms, and gaffs using knots as illustrated. If you wish to use your own technique of tying, remember that these small pieces must be able to move after they are attached to the mast, to permit the completed assembly to pass through the mouth of the bottle.

Now take a short length of your No. 30 gauge wire, push it through the bottom hole in the mast and bend the ends down to form a "U" shape. The two ends should project ³⁄₁₆ inch below the mast base. This will form the pivot point for the mast.

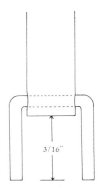

3/16"

Base of mast showing wire pivot point

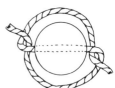

Knots for tying the spars

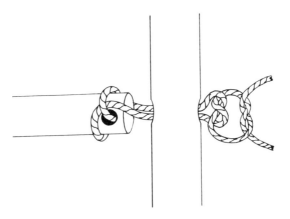

Attaching spars to the mast

Mark the position of the mast on the deck of the ship and drill two holes with your No. 75 drill point where the ends of the pivot wire touch the deck. Slide the ends of the wire into the holes and check to see that the mast pivots on the wire until it almost parallels the deck. Check your spars for free movement. They should be able to turn parallel to the axis of the hull also.

Now, set the masts in their places on the deck. Attach your fore-and-aft stays at the appropriate points using clove hitches. Run the stays through the various holes in the masts and through the hull and bowsprit as indicated on your plans. Leave at least 18 inches of thread beyond the bowsprit for later use in erecting the masts. A few thumb tacks pushed into the base of the workstand will provide a handy place to wind the excess thread to avoid tangles.

Checking the mast pivot

If you have a line which runs between two masts that is fastened *at both ends*, be sure that the line ties at a higher point on the forward mast than on the after. When the masts are lowered, the distance between any two points on the masts increases in the direction of the lowering. A tie which runs from low forward to high aft will almost immediately break or stop the backward movement of the masts as you lower.

Be careful, too, where you have the stays enter or fasten to the masts. All entry and tie points should be located above the various yards and booms so that they will not interfere with the sails, when they are later fitted into place.

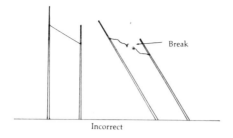

Incorrect

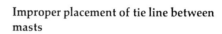

Improper placement of tie line between masts

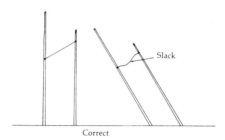

Correct

Proper placement of tie line between masts

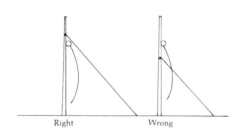

Right　　　　Wrong

Location of tie and penetration point of stays on square-rigged masts

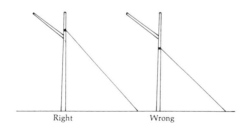

Right　　　　Wrong

Location of tie and penetration point of stays on fore-and-aft-rigged masts.

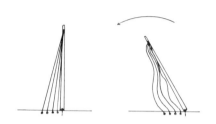

Proper shroudline placement in bulwarks

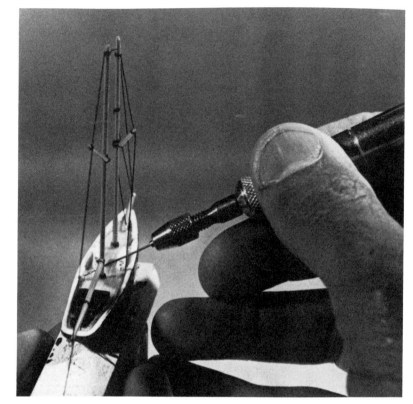

Positioning the first shroud hole alongside the mast

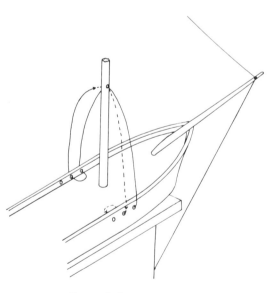

General plan of threading the shrouds

You are now ready to drill the holes in the bulwarks for attaching the shroudlines. These are the small lines that support the mast on either side. Use your No. 75 drill. Remember that none of your shroudlines can run from the mast forward, or the mast will not be able to fold back when you are ready to slide your ship into the bottle. You can avoid this problem by drilling your first two holes on either side of your ship directly beside the mast. Then, drill each successive hole further aft, keeping a minimum space of 2 millimeters between holes to prevent splitting.

To rig the shrouds, take a length of No. 60 thread about 18 inches long; tie a knot in one end and thread through the forward hole on the starboard side from inside to out. Pull all the thread through until the knot stops at the hole. Next, run the thread through the proper hole in the mast, down the exterior of the port side of the hull, and into the first hole on that side. Guide the thread aft inside the bulwarks to the next hole, where you repeat the sequence until all threading is complete. Keep a slight forward strain on your mast to hold it in place as you tighten the shroudlines. When you are satisfied that the mast is correctly positioned, and all shrouds are tight, "tie" your shroudline by applying a coat of nail polish to the thread, inside and out, where it passes through the hull. Finally, trim the excess thread and repeat the pro-

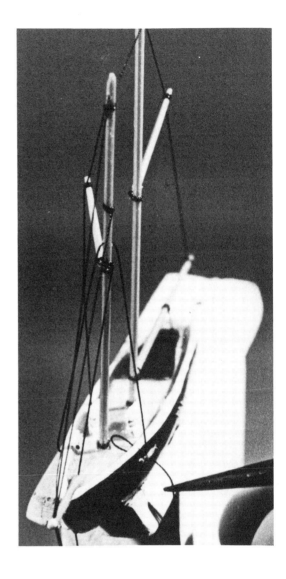

Out the second shroud hole on the port side

Threading the first shroud

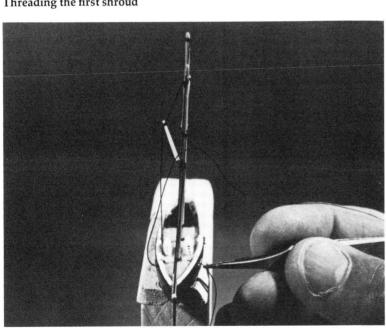

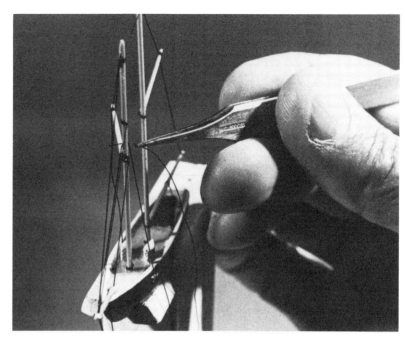

Back through the same hole in the mast

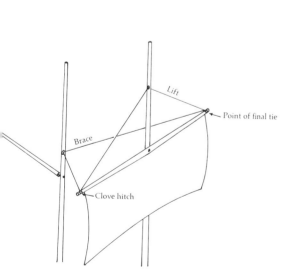

General plan for lifts and braces

In the diagram: Lift, Brace, Point of final tie, Clove hitch

The rigging completed

cedure with the next mast. When all of your shroudlines are in place, touch up the enamel on the sides of the hull so that the drill holes are covered. Check again to be certain that all of your masts still fold down without binding.

Had you chosen to build a ship with square sails you would now rig the lifts and braces which hold the yards in place. Begin on the starboard side and tie a clove hitch as close to the end of the yard as possible. Again, seal it in place with a drop of polish. Now follow your plans for this rigging and pass the ends of the thread through the proper holes so that they both end at the port side of the

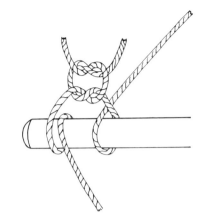

Tying off lifts and braces

A square-rigged ship with rigging completed

Leaḃaċlanna Ċonnḋae Poṙtláiṙġe

yards. Here they are tied off as indicated in the diagram. When you are finished, the yard should be able to move up and down and fore and aft just as it does on a real ship. Sufficient tension should exist on the lines to hold the yard in any set position.

When all of your rigging has been completed you are ready to cut and attach your sails.

THE SAILS

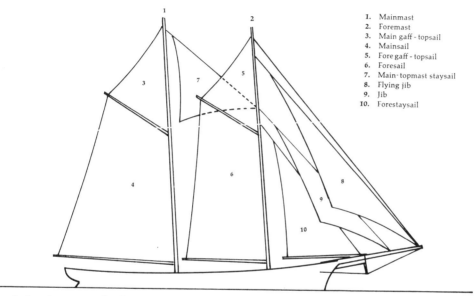

1. Mainmast
2. Foremast
3. Main gaff - topsail
4. Mainsail
5. Fore gaff - topsail
6. Foresail
7. Main-topmast staysail
8. Flying jib
9. Jib
10. Forestaysail

Sail plan for a typical schooner

Your sails are best made from a piece of medium weight bond paper. Although some old-timers used starched cloth sails on the earliest models, the disproportionate size of the weave tends to rob the little ship of an authentic appearance. Other negative factors are the problems in marking seam lines and reef points, unraveling of the edges; a tendency to resist curling; and bulkiness. Bond paper offers none of the above difficulties, and you can give it a slightly aged look by soaking the white paper in warm coffee for half an hour. Lay the paper on a flat surface to dry and then press it flat with an iron.

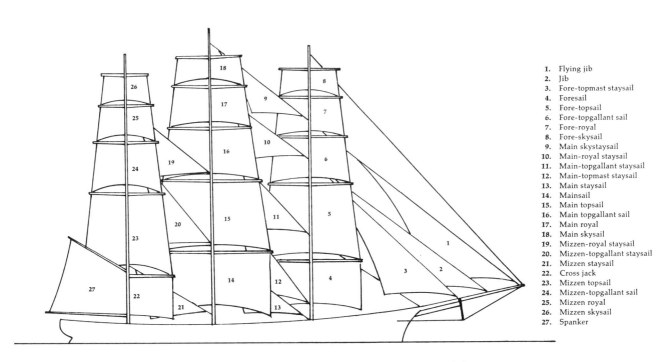

1. Flying jib
2. Jib
3. Fore-topmast staysail
4. Foresail
5. Fore-topsail
6. Fore-topgallant sail
7. Fore-royal
8. Fore-skysail
9. Main skystaysail
10. Main-royal staysail
11. Main-topgallant staysail
12. Main-topmast staysail
13. Main staysail
14. Mainsail
15. Main topsail
16. Main topgallant sail
17. Main royal
18. Main skysail
19. Mizzen-royal staysail
20. Mizzen-topgallant staysail
21. Mizzen staysail
22. Cross jack
23. Mizzen topsail
24. Mizzen-topgallant sail
25. Mizzen royal
26. Mizzen skysail
27. Spanker

Sail plan for a typical square-rigged ship

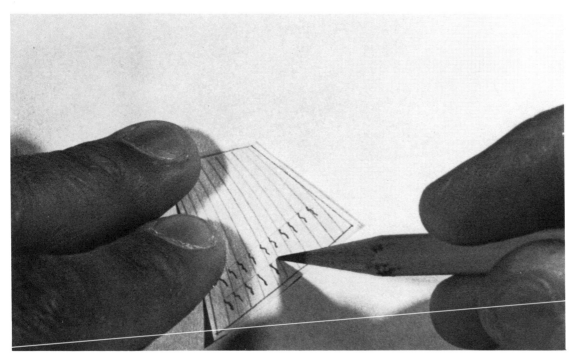

Marking seams and reef points on the sail

Curving the sail around a pencil

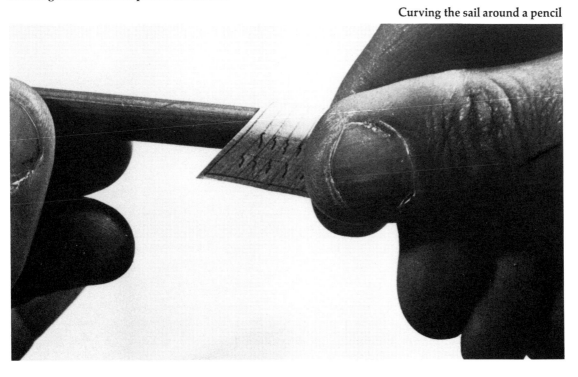

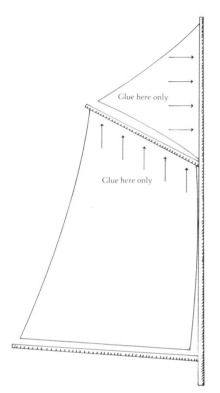

Gluing edges for gaff-rigged sails

Glue here only

Glue here only

Glue along edges
and in center only,
to allow sail
to move up
and down stay.

Glue

Gluing points for staysails and jibs

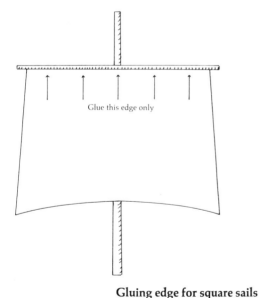

Glue this edge only

Gluing edge for square sails

Measure and lay out your sails one by one according to the plan provided. As each sail is cut to size hold it in position on the ship to be certain of the fit.

Take a sharp No. 2 pencil and lightly indicate the seam lines and reef points on both sides of the sail. These small lines can be put on free hand and add a great deal to the final authentic appearance of the model.

Before gluing it in place give each sail a slight curve to make it appear that the wind is blowing against it. The easiest way to do this is to wrap the sail around a pencil.

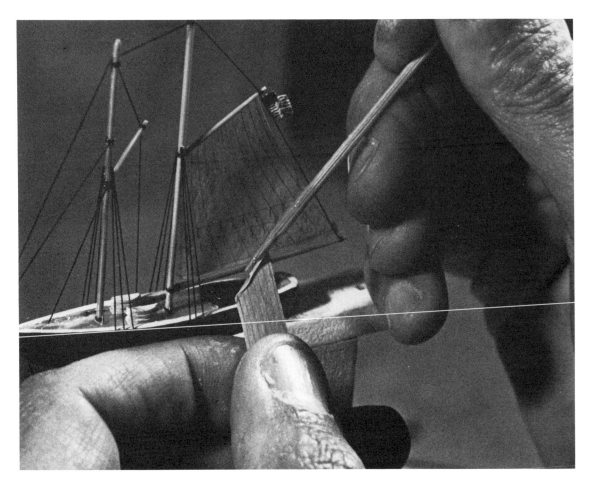

Applying clear polish to the edge of a sail with a sliver of bamboo

The sails are glued in place with clear nail polish sparingly applied. Before gluing each sail, check to be certain which edge is to be glued. Sails that attach to the spars are glued along one edge only, otherwise the mast will not fold back. For the same reason, the staysails and jibs are not glued to their respective fore-and-aft lines but are glued around them so they are free to slide up and down. Fold the staysails and jibs over the fore-and-aft lines on the ship and apply glue in the center and along the outer edges only. Check to make sure you re-

The completed model

tain the curve in the sails when you press the two sides together.

With the sails attached, your small vessel is practically finished. For the final touch dab a speck of white paint on the tips of the spars for emphasis and, if you have made one, glue on a flag. That does it! You are ready to slide your ship into the bottle.

PLACING THE SHIP
INTO THE BOTTLE

Retrieve your bottle from where the "sea" has been drying and apply a layer of white glue to the previously prepared bed for your ship. An easy way to do this is to suck
some white glue into one end of a straw. Put your thumb
over the other end and place the tip of the straw in the

Inserting white glue with a straw

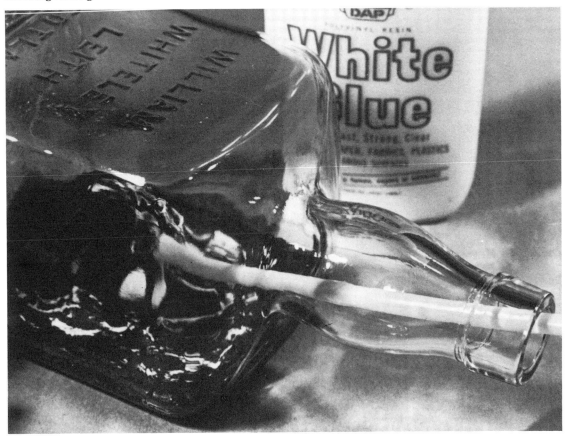

Masts down and ready for the bottle

Sliding into the mouth of the bottle

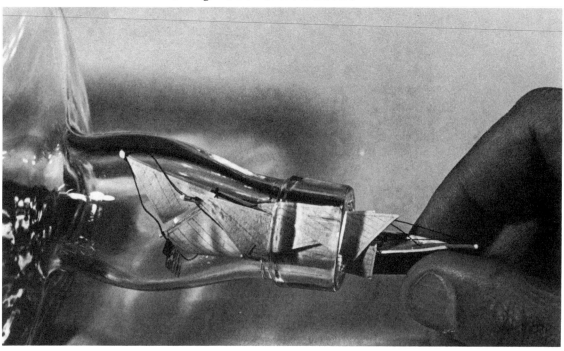

**Raising sails inside the bottle while
holding the model with ten-inch tweezers**

indented area. Release your thumb and the glue will run
out. The glue is transparent when dry, so add enough so
that it will squeeze up around the ship once it is in place.

While the ship is still attached to the workstand,
release the fore-and-aft lines from where you have se-
cured them to the stand and gently lower your masts.
Begin with your aft mast and work forward, being careful not to crush your sails. Gently move the various spars
so that they are reasonably parallel to the hull. Let the
sails project over the side.

Now, remove the ship from the stand, roll any projecting sails around the hull, and slide the ship, stern first,

Model glued in place—masts erect

two-thirds of the way into the mouth of the bottle. Take a firm grip on the forward portion of the hull with your 10 inch tweezers and slide the ship the remaining distance into the main cavity of the bottle.

With the ship well inside the bottle, but still held by the tweezers, raise your masts. You will want the sails and rigging clear of the hull when you press your ship into the bed of glue. (It's possible that you could encounter some tangles in the rigging, but these can be straightened out once you've settled your model in its bed by using the positioning wire.)

Now ease your model into its bed in the wet glue and withdraw the tweezers. Using a piece of bent wire, press down on the deck and push the model solidly into position. Don't despair if you now notice something wrong that requires getting the ship back out of the bottle. The only real difficulty is the clean-up job before you can proceed again. The glue smears all along the neck of the bottle and requires several swabs with a wet Kleenex on a wire before it is cleared out. If you're finally satisfied with everything, give the vessel a slight heel away from the wind for realism and set the bottle aside to dry overnight.

It's fairly important that you line the ship up with

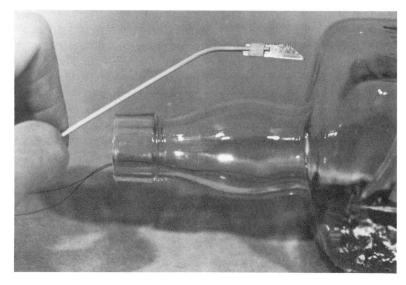

the axis of the bottle, or you will introduce the problem
of an off-center pull on the bowsprit when you erect the
masts. Since the bowsprit is a very slender piece of wood
which has been further weakened by drilling holes in it
you risk probable breakage. Breakage at this point is
tragic since the ship has already been glued firmly in the
bed and must be torn free to repair.

The final step, once the glue is set, is to permanently
secure your masts in the upright position. Pull each of the
projecting threads until you are satisfied that the masts
are completely raised. Keep tension on the projecting
lines and tape them tightly to the outside of the bottle.
Then, using a thin piece of wood or wire apply a drop
of clear nail polish at each point where the stays pass
through the bowsprit. Allow at least thirty minutes for
the drying process and then, *before cutting away the excess thread*, release the taped lines to be certain that the
masts remain upright.

Now, cut away the excess thread beneath the bowsprit with a small piece of razor blade attached to a thin
stick.

Your last task before sealing the bottle is to arrange
the sails in a realistic conformation with the positioning
wire.

SEALING AND
FINISHING
THE BOTTLE

Seal the bottle with a snug-fitting cork pushed in about ¼ inch and cut it off flush with the glass. Sealing wax will complete the job. The easiest way to apply it is to melt a stick of wax against a piece of hot metal and let it drip onto the cork. A soldering iron is perfect for the job. The

Melting sealing wax onto the cork

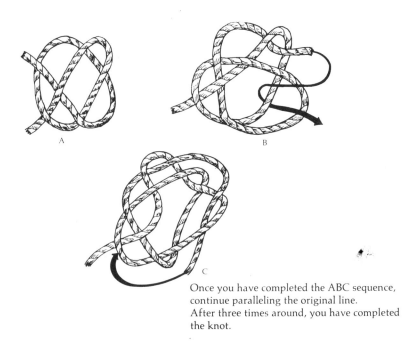

Once you have completed the ABC sequence,
continue paralleling the original line.
After three times around, you have completed
the knot.

Weaving a Turk's-Head knot

Labeling on the underside of the bottle

melted wax won't harden too rapidly, so wait until you have covered the entire end of the bottle before pressing the wax flat with a knife blade. If you have a small anchor or similar nautical emblem press the design into the hot wax for added effect. (I have used designs from buttons, medals, and jewelry.) You can also transfer some of the designs in these pages to a linoleum block and carve your own die, perhaps incorporating your initials. If you have chosen a screw-top bottle for your ship you should cover the glass threads with sealing wax as well.

As a final nautical touch, decorate the neck of the bottle with a "Turk's-Head" knot woven out of ⅛ inch cotton fishing line. Follow the plan for the "Turk's-Head" which is provided. It requires 4 feet of line and a few minutes of practice. Once you complete the basic knot, just follow the line round and round until you have three strands side by side. Be sure to dip the ends of the line into your clear nail polish to provide a good leader.

I am certain you will want to label your work with your name, the date, the name of the ship, and perhaps other data. An easy way to accomplish this is to thin a bit of white enamel and write the information on the base of the bottle with an old fashioned pen point. If you are more ambitious, cut yourself a small disk of copper slightly smaller than the size of the cork. Buff it smooth and have a jeweler engrave the information on its face. This will cost you a few dollars, but if you have built an attractive model the slight cost will be well worth it. Heat the copper slightly and then press it firmly into the sealing wax covering the cork. Finally, rub some black paint into the design to provide contrast and emphasize the lettering.

Labeling on the end of the bottle

The completed job

BUILDING
A DISPLAY
STAND

Some form of stand or base is almost a requirement for displaying ships-in-bottles. Even flat-sided bottles look more distinctive on a base of polished mahogany, and round bottles need a mount to prevent rolling and to insure that the sea is level and the masts upright.

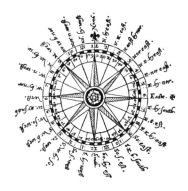

When planning your stand remember that simplicity is an asset. An elaborate and over-decorated stand could detract from the simple beauty of your ship model. Use traditional materials in construction such as wood and rope and avoid plexiglass and plastics, which are more suitable for airplane models.

Generally speaking you can build your model stand for a flat surface such as a table top, desk, or mantelpiece; or you can build a stand which permits the model to be hung on the wall. The illustrations which accompany this chapter will provide you with some basic ideas you can alter to suit your needs. No matter what type of stand you plan it is important to remember that the secret to an attractive display lies in design balance. The bottled ship, the stand, and the materials you use should all complement one another so that nothing is overpowering or distracting. Never forget that your ship model is the feature you wish to display. Beautiful woodcarving on the stand is fine, but if it distracts from the model it should not be used.

Because of the problem of achieving an overall apparent balance I prefer a stand which extends slightly beyond each end of the bottle. Shorter cradles are adequate for the job and are used frequently, but I always feel uncomfortable with them. When I plan a stand for the normal 11 to 12 inch bottle, I usually allow for a ¾ inch overhang at each end. This, of course, can vary with the length.

The width of your base will be determined by the type of bottle you plan to mount. If you have a bottle which rests on a flat base, allow about a ½ inch of exposed wood along the sides. If your bottle is round, make your base the same width as the diameter of the bottle. The curvature of a round bottle will permit a sufficient expanse of wood to show.

Keep the thickness of your base in proportion to your other dimensions. For a standard bottle a base thickness of ¾ inch is about correct, so use no more than that unless you are working with a much larger bottle. Smaller bottles require a base which appears less heavy.

There are many types of wood from which to choose. Factors such as availability, cost, and ease of working must all be considered when making your selection. Clear pine is a readily available, inexpensive, and easily worked wood which can be stained to almost any desired shade. Mahogany is a more nautical material which finishes well and possesses an excellent color of its own. Teak is another beautiful nautical wood, but it is expensive and difficult to work because of its extremely high mineral content. I am told that Scandinavian craftsmen who work in this material are paid a premium over their regular wages to compensate for the excessive wear on their tools.

Once you have built your stand, finish the wood as you would any fine piece of carpentry. If you wish an opaque finish there are antiquing kits on the market today which can create a very authentic aged appearance in a variety of hues. For clear finishes there are various varnishes and epoxies available. Or if you wish to avoid

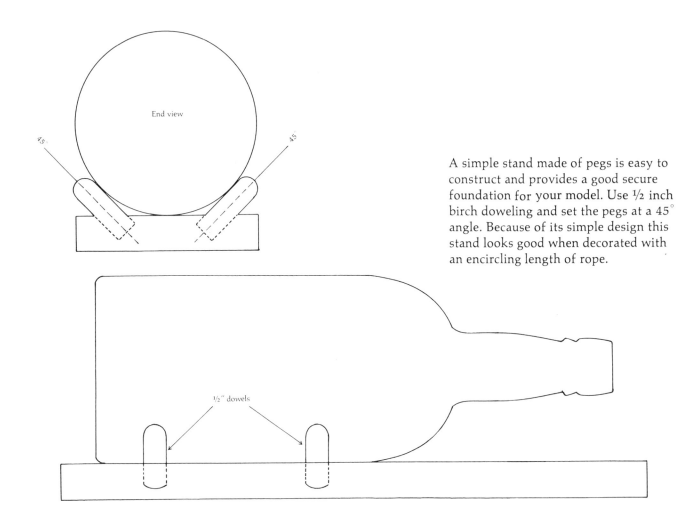

End view

45°   45°

A simple stand made of pegs is easy to construct and provides a good secure foundation for your model. Use ½ inch birch doweling and set the pegs at a 45° angle. Because of its simple design this stand looks good when decorated with an encircling length of rope.

½" dowels

Simple peg support

the bother of drying times and multiple coats you might want to consider using a simple wax finish. I make an effective mixture by melting an ounce or so of beeswax into a cup of heated turpentine. After the turpentine has cooled I mix in a teaspoonful of neat's-foot oil, which acts as a penetrating agent. The completed mixture is applied to the wood and permitted to dry; then it is buffed gently with a soft cloth. For very porous woods repeat the application several times until a smooth, even finish is achieved.

A stand of this type can be made by mortising three pieces of ¾ inch board together. By changing the dimensions of the center board the length of the stand can be varied to suit the bottle. When planning a stand of this type be sure to set the bottle down at least ½ inch into the base to insure a firm hold. The side of this stand offers a convenient spot for a brass identification plate.

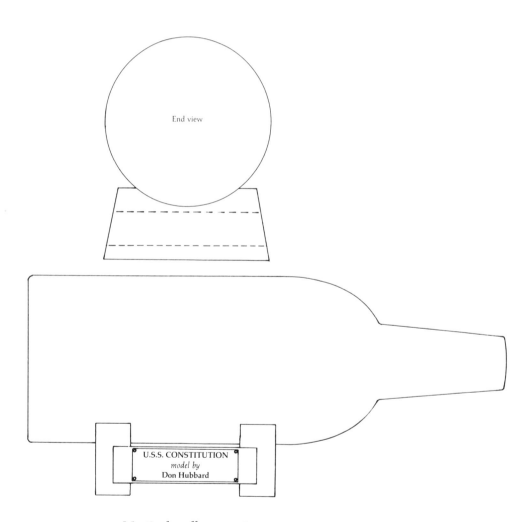

End view

U.S.S. CONSTITUTION
model by
Don Hubbard

Mortised cradle support

Though slightly more difficult to build, this stand offers a more secure foundation than any of the others. The base of the bottle is firmly anchored in a wooden disk which has been chiseled out to a depth of ¼ inch for this purpose. The neck of the bottle is held in place by attaching the free ends of the line used in making the Turk's-Head knot to a brass cleat.

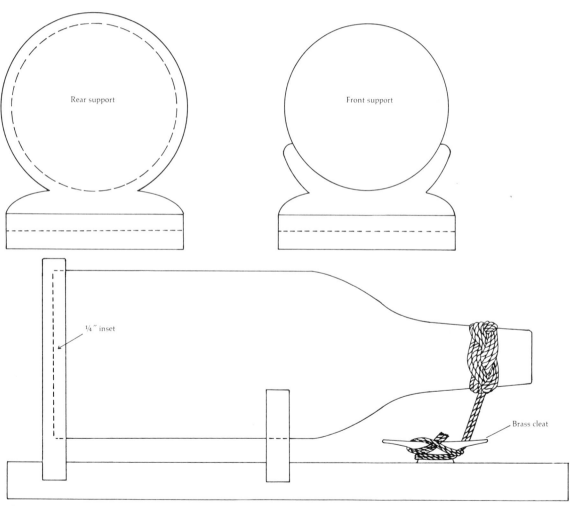

Rear support

Front support

¼″ inset

Brass cleat

Cleat and base support

Leaḃarlanna Connoje Portláinge

Decorative ropework may be added around the perimeter of the stand after the finish has been applied to the wood. Standard Manila rope may be used, but I prefer the new nylon ropes which are now widely available. Just to be sure there is no mistake, I am referring to nylon ropes which have been made strand by strand in the traditional way, rather than the braided kind sometimes found in marine hardware stores. The advantages I find that nylon has over Manila are that it tends to resist soiling and is more supple, and its individual fibers are less apt to break and cause an untidy appearance.

You should select a piece of rope which has a diameter compatible with the thickness of your wooden base. For a wood thickness of ¾ inch a rope diameter of ½ inch is about correct. Carefully measure your rope so that the ends will exactly meet after encircling the stand, and then cut and whip the ends to prevent unraveling. To avoid later problems with rust, fasten the rope around the stand with brass or copper nails. These should be tapped into the wood sufficiently far to bury their heads among the strands of the rope. Cover the two whipped ends where they meet with a Turk's-Head knot woven to the proper circumference.

If your stand is designed to rest on a flat surface, it is a good idea to use some form of felt protective pad on the underside. Small, circular, adhesive-backed pads designed for this purpose can be obtained in many variety stores.

Ships-in-bottles have an almost universal appeal, and they almost unfailingly attract attention. They are also quite small and difficult to view at a distance, so it is only a kindness to your guests to position your model where it can be viewed with relative ease. If you mount the model on a wall, put it at proper eye level for viewing. If it is intended for a desk or other flat surface, keep it where it is accessible and where your friends can examine it in comfort. People should be able to gather around the model while you explain details of construction and rig-

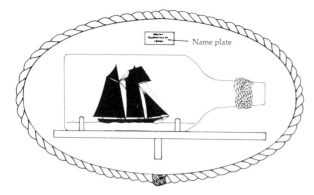

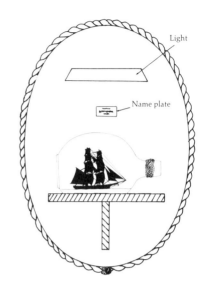

ing and describe the technique of inserting the tiny vessel into the bottle.

Suitable lighting always should be provided. If your model is wall-mounted, the small lamps used by museums to illuminate paintings are ideal and inexpensive. These can be built right into your wall-mount or hung independently. For table-top models you can use a small Tensor lamp for illumination. In addition to the aid they provide in viewing, small individual lamps also tend to spotlight the model and add a dramatic effect.

If you wish to do greatest justice to your model, locate it so that it is not in competition with other works of art. It is distracting to surround it with bits of scrimshaw, paintings of ships, and other nautical odds and ends. You should have no qualms on this score, for a ship-in-a-bottle can easily stand alone.

Finally, use good judgment if children are frequent visitors or are part of the household. I have mentioned that ships-in-bottles have universal appeal, and that includes the youngsters. Who can blame a little guy if in his enthusiasm he knocks a small bottled ship off a table? If children are a part of the complex, then it is only fair to place your work of art somewhere where it will be out of reach. Let them look at it, but only with an adult supervising.

You should strive to make your ship-in-a-bottle a primary attraction wherever you place it. If you do, the friendly enthusiasm it generates will quickly have you back at the workbench patiently planning and building your next miniature ship.

Wall mounts

These illustrations show two variations in wall mounts for ships-in-bottles. Because of weight considerations the backboard thickness on these mounts should be no more than ½ inch. A heavy duty bracket is a necessity when hanging these boards.

PREPARATION
OF PLANS

The ability to prepare your own plans is the final ingredient needed to become a successful master of ship-in-bottle art. Library shelves abound with books full of illustrations of sailing ships. These are yours to duplicate in reduced three-dimensional scale once you have learned the technique. You become free to roam through the ages building models of everything from the simple square-rigged long boats of the intrepid Vikings to the magnificent clipper ships of the 19th century.

Viking long boat

One of the major assets of producing your own plans is that you can obtain an amazingly accurate scale model by mathematically reducing or enlarging your illustration. To achieve the greatest accuracy on your first attempts, select the most direct side view you can find of the ship you wish to copy. It is possible to make a reasonably accurate model from a quartering view of your selected ship, but your ability to compensate for the foreshortening of the hull length in this type of illustration is heavily dependent upon both good fortune and your basic knowledge of the general proportions of ships. Since direct side views of sailing vessels are not hard to find it is far wiser to select one of these for your initial efforts.

Your burdens will be further eased if you take your measurements using a rule with a millimeter scale. You will benefit not only from the mathematical ease of using the metric system, but also from the generally smaller gradations. If a millimeter scale is not available, it is possible to use an inch scale if you disregard the inch breakdown and record all of your measurements in sixteenths or thirty-seconds. This is a more time-consuming but workable procedure.

The basic technique of proportional reduction or enlargement is simple and depends upon the correct establishment of a scale relationship between the hull size of your illustration and the desired hull size of your finished model. Once this basic ratio has been established you can easily reduce or enlarge the measurements from your illustration by proportional mathematics. For example, suppose we wish to compute the mainmast height (M) of our model. If we establish a model hull length (H) of 70 millimeters versus an illustration hull length (I) of 110 millimeters, and if the mainmast height (M^1) in our illustration is 98 millimeters, then using the formula $\frac{M}{M^1} = \frac{H}{I}$ we can compute the unknown dimensions of our model mainmast. Let's take the figures and work it out:

$$\frac{M}{98} = \frac{70}{110}$$

$$M = \frac{98 \times 70}{110}$$

Model mainmast height $= 62.4$

If you have a slide rule you can set up your basic ratio and read the final answer directly above the figure which represents the measurement in your illustration.

Naturally the overall size of your model will depend upon the basic decision which establishes your model hull size. This, in turn, will be a function of the size of the bottle you have chosen. I generally select a length of 65 to 75 millimeters for the hull, exclusive of the bowsprit or the overhang of the boom. When these two measurements are included in the calculations the overall length will have grown to about 100 millimeters. This fills a standard bottle nicely, and still leaves sufficient room for the ship to "sail." Smaller models are too difficult to work on, and larger models will require taller masts, which may not fit inside the bottle you have chosen.

Once you understand the workings of the proportion formula you can establish the remaining measurements for your model so that you can construct a working drawing to scale. As a minimum you will need measurements of mast heights; gaffs and booms; bowsprit and jib boom; the positioning of the masts on the deck in relation to the bow and stern; the heights of the gaffs, booms, and yards above the deck; and any other obvious features which you will wish to record in scale.

With the data gathered you can make an accurate scale drawing of your ship. Begin by drawing a waterline and measuring off the length of your basic hull. Draw light vertical lines from these points as guides, and then draw in the curve or "sheer" of the deck about 5 to 6 millimeters above the waterline amidships. The hull will slope upwards slightly at the bow and stern and will be generally level amidships. Since all ships vary in deck curvature this is one of several points where you must rely upon your own judgment and artistic abilities. It is helpful, nevertheless, to use a French Curve to plot this deck sheer.

Draw in the bow and stern configuration as closely as you can from your illustration. Again, a French Curve can be quite helpful in accurately recording these shapes. Drop the lines of both bow and stern below the waterline about 2 millimeters and join these points with a straight base line. This portion of your hull will lie in the depression in your putty sea when you later put your ship into the bottle.

With the side elevation of your hull complete, measure off and draw in all of the other features whose size and position you have determined. To some degree, again, you must rely on your judgment to determine whether all of your features are positioned correctly and resemble the ship in your illustration. In small scale an inaccuracy of 1 or 2 millimeters can mean the difference between a

Arabian dhow

pleasing and a grotesque representation of your ship. Note especially if there is any fore-and-aft rake to the masts, and try to copy carefully the angle at which the bowsprit juts upward.

With the drawing of the main features of your model complete, draw in your shroudlines to correspond as closely as possible with those shown in the original illustration. However, as we mentioned in an earlier chapter, it is important that all of these shrouds terminate in the bulwarks *aft* of the supported mast so that it will be free to pivot backwards for clearance through the mouth of the bottle.

The shrouds should not penetrate the mast too closely to other holes which must be drilled for the gaffs, booms, yards, or stays or the mast will become weakened at these points. You will note from the plans in this book that the various mast holes which must be bored are separated by about 2 millimeters or more.

Drawing in the fore-and-aft stays also requires some thought. Begin by copying the run of the stays as they appear in your illustration. Now modify these so that your masts will be able to pivot backwards without binding. If you have a stay which runs between two masts, and it is fastened at both ends so that it cannot run free, it must be fastened much higher on the forward mast than on the after mast, or the mast will not drop completely to the horizontal.

It is also imperative that your stays enter or attach to the various masts just *above* the yards of your square sails. If they enter or attach below the yards they will interfere with the hang of the sails when they are later placed in position.

Finally, clearly indicate on your drawing which stays will run through the mast and where they will penetrate the hull and bowsprit, so that later they may be used to erect the masts after the ship is in the bottle.

If you have selected a ship which has square sails, your next job will be to determine the size of the individual yards. In all probability your illustration does not accurately represent these, and you must rely upon a certain amount of guesswork to complete your drawing. The easiest approach is to estimate the length of the various yards, beginning with the main yard, which is the largest, and proceed to the smaller yards of the topmasts. As an easy rule of thumb make the main yard equal to one-half the length of the hull and scale down the remaining yards from there. Even the smallest of the yards should be no shorter than the beam of the ship's hull.

You can portray your yards on the drawing that you have already made, or you may draw each mast separately and indicate the yards on these. For ships of two masts or less I find it fairly simple to follow my plans when everything is shown in one drawing. However, when I have more than two masts it sometimes simplifies matters to represent the yards on a separate drawing together with an indication of the holes which must be drilled.

Your final drawing should be a plan view of the hull looking down from aloft. Once again, begin with a straight centerline and draw two parallel outside lines to represent the straight sides of the ship, or the maximum beam if the ship is short with a curving gunwale. Your beam should be no greater than about one-half the diameter of the neck of your bottle in order to permit the ship to pass through with all of its rigging.

Indicate the overall length of the hull along your centerline, and then draw in the curvature of the gunwales as closely as you are able. Once again, you must base your estimate of what this should be on your knowledge of ships of the type you have chosen. Use a French Curve to facilitate accuracy and clean rendition.

With the overall drawing accomplished, add scale representations of details which you intend to include. These can vary from deckhouses and ship's boats to winches, hatches, and other small items. Next, carefully indicate the positions of the masts on the deck.

Your final job will be to show the shape and size of the sails which your ship will carry. Don't spend too much time on this, for I have found that the finished ship will differ in minor ways from the scale drawing and that, as a result, I usually have to recut the sails to fit the actual model. All you really need is an indication of the overall plan. On ships with fore-and-aft sails I usually indicate my sail plan lightly on the side-view drawing of the ship. On the square-riggers I trace out the square sail plan on the drawing of the yards, and that of the fore-and-aft sails on the side elevation.

You should now be able to prepare your own plans from illustrations of old sailing ships, and you will have opened for yourself a whole new field of opportunity to create original works of ship-in-bottle art. With a knowledge of scale reduction procedure you will be able to create almost exact replicas of ancient ships in a way totally unknown to the 19th century forecastle scrimshaw artist. You will have achieved mastery of an art form which combines the best of both old and new procedures. From here it is up to you, and I will take my leave by wishing you "fair winds and a following sea" in your future efforts at ship-in-bottle art.

PLANS FOR OTHER SHIP MODELS

Brig in a Pinch Bottle

Baltimore Clipper

For the model builder who lacks the time to work out his own drawings I have included scaled plans of several different and interesting sailing vessels of a variety of types. Some of these vessels were famous as individual ships and others are noteworthy for the part the vessel type played in the history of seafaring. All make excellent and showy models for ship-in-bottle art. Depending on the level of skill you have developed you can select a plan of almost any degree of complexity from those offered.

Plan for Schooner Yacht America
Scale 1:1

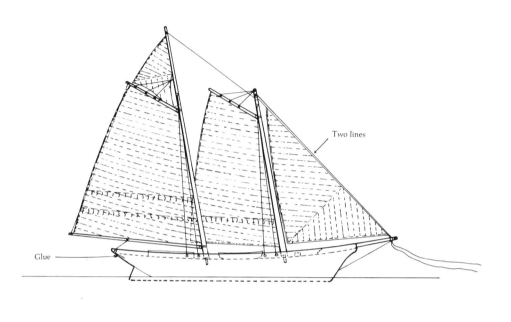

Two lines

Glue

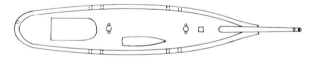

History—Schooner Yacht *America*—The *America* was a racing yacht designed along the lines of the speedy pilot schooners. She was launched at New York in 1851 to compete in a race with 14 English yachts around the Isle of Wight. Victory in this race earned her the possession of the "America's Cup," which has since become the object of a series of world-renowned competitions in the waters off Newport, Rhode Island.

Color scheme—Black hull, white trim on rails and spar tips. Completely white gaffs and booms. White deckhouses.

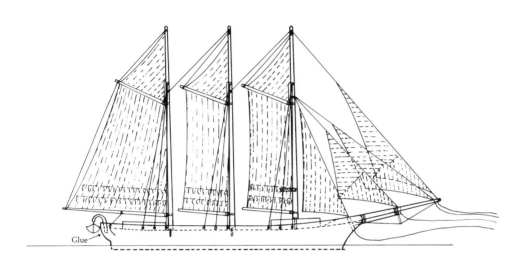

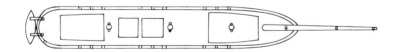

History—Coastal Schooner—Schooners of this type played the major role in transporting bulk commodities along both coasts of the United States during the 1800s. Schooners were popular because they could be handled with smaller crews than the more complicated square-rigged vessels. The number of masts on coastal schooners varied from two to six, with one seven–master, the *Thomas W. Lawson*, but most coastal schooners were three-masted vessels. A few coastal schooners were still in service through the 1930s, but the coastal trade finally died out with the onset of World War II.

Color scheme—Black or dark brown hull. White rails and spar tips. Brown deckhouses and hatches. White life boat. Port and starboard lights dark red and green respectively.

Plan for Baltimore Clipper

Scale 1:1

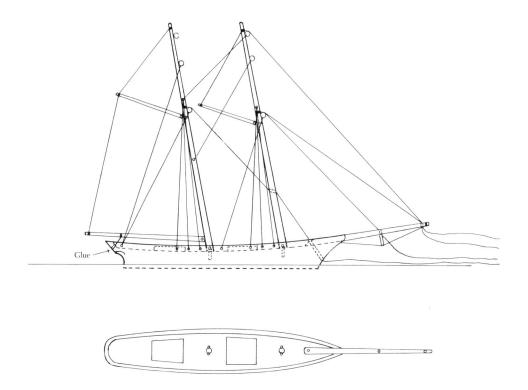

Glue

History—Baltimore Clipper—The Baltimore Clipper was designed to meet the needs of its time. During colonial days and following the American Revolution, Yankee ships were forbidden to enter many foreign ports and were preyed upon by warships and privateers of the European nations. To engage in any kind of commerce many American seafarers had to become smugglers and rely upon speed to avoid capture. Chesapeake Bay shipbuilders therefore evolved the design known as the Baltimore Clipper—a topsail schooner with a mass of canvas and a slender, deep-draft hull to help her sail closer to the wind than her pursuers. Because of their speed these vessels made excellent privateers and became famous in that role during the Revolution and the War of 1812. In peacetime they lost favor to vessels with larger holds, but their slim, sharp lines were later embodied in the famous "Clipper Ships" of the 1840–1860 era.

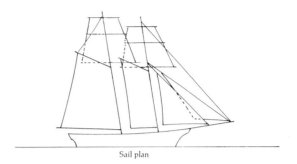

Sail plan

Main

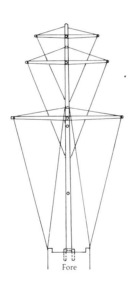

Fore

Color scheme—Dark brown hull, white trim on rails, dark brown deckhouses.

Plan for Brigantine
Scale 1:1

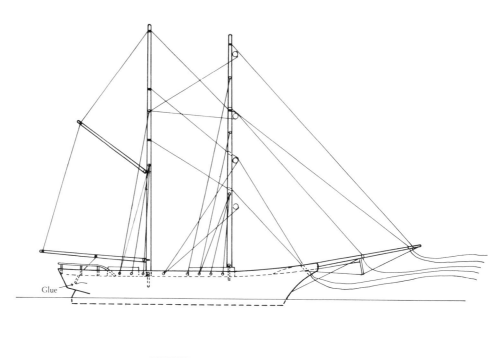

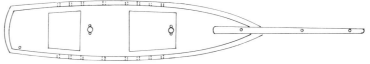

Glue

History—Brigantine—The brigantine, sometimes called the hermaphrodite brig, was a swift, seaworthy vessel easily handled by a small crew. Because of these qualities this type of vessel became a favorite in the maritime trade for almost two centuries. When mounted with guns the trim brigantine was also popular as a privateer, and many of them served as such during the American Revolution and the War of 1812.

Color scheme—Black hull, white trim on rails and tips of spars. Brown deckhouses. If you're making your model a privateer, add a white stripe down the side and paint on eight black gun ports.

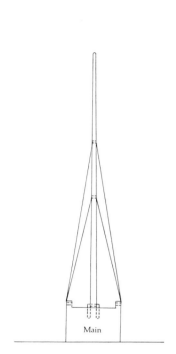

Main

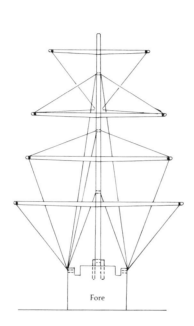

Fore

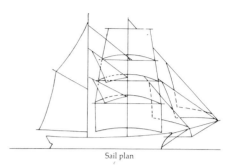

Sail plan

Plan for U.S.S. Constitution
Scale 1:1

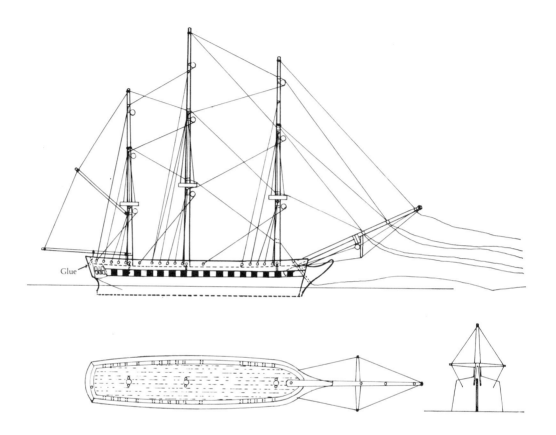

Glue

History—U.S.S. *Constitution*—One of a series of fast, graceful, heavily canvased vessels authorized by Congress in 1794 to combat the depredations of Barbary pirates against U.S. merchantmen. These vessels were ship-rigged and stoutly built and were termed frigates—sailing warships of more than 24 and less than 50 guns. American ships of this class were so superbly built and handled, and the gunnery was so keen, that many British captains during the War of 1812 believed them to be disguised ships of the line carrying 50 guns or more. The *Constitution* was launched in 1797 and served the U.S. as an active warship for 84 years. She survives today as a symbol of the early U.S. Navy and may be seen at the Boston Navy Yard.

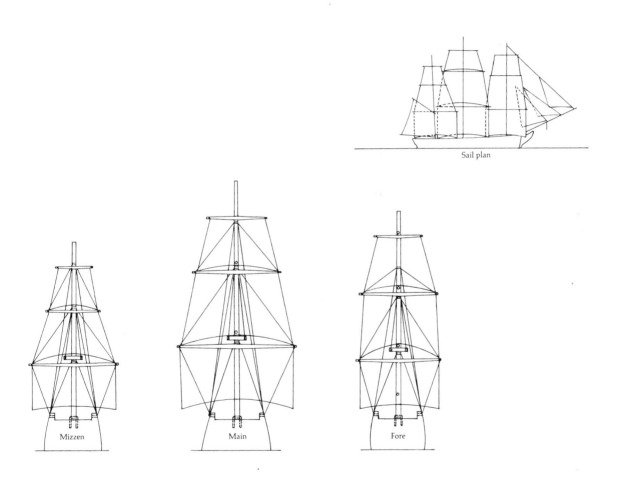

Sail plan

Mizzen

Main

Fore

Color scheme—Black hull, white stripe down the side, with 16 black gun ports evenly spaced.

Plan for Galleon
Scale 1:1

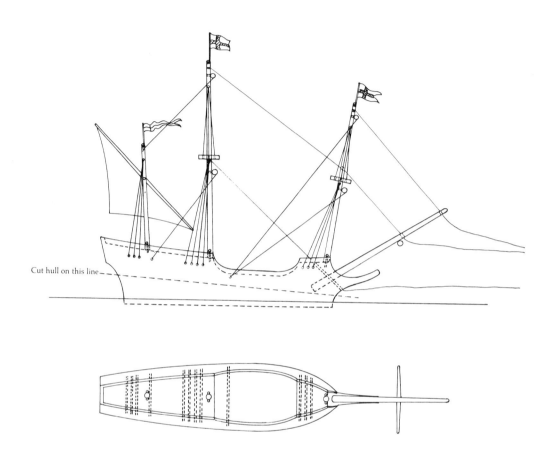

Cut hull on this line

History—Galleon—The galleon appears to have descended from the earlier, more cumbersome, carrack. Galleons differ from carracks in having a much-reduced forecastle and a projecting point on the bow called a beak head. Galleons were also built on more slender lines, being approximately three times as long as they were wide rather than two times as for carracks. Whatever their origin the type had become very popular among seafaring nations by the middle of the 16th century and remained so for over 150 years.

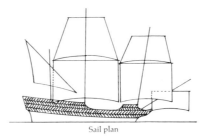

Sail plan

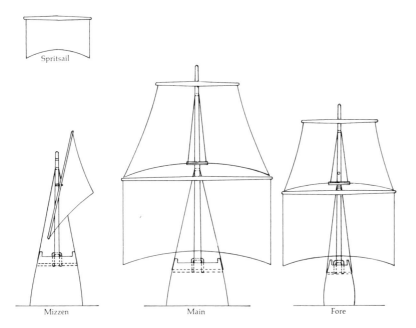

Spritsail

Mizzen   Main   Fore

Color scheme—Contemporary paintings of these vessels often show them brightly decorated along the raised portions of the hull, indicated by hachured marks on the small Sail plan. Various combinations of colors were employed, such as alternating red and white or red and blue stripes running the length of the ship. The markings often represented the family colors or indicated the position of the owner. Warships carried the colors of the country or the king. To obtain other ideas for color schemes, the model builder should visit his local library to examine illustrations of ships of this era.

Special instructions on following page.

Special instructions—Because of its raised after deck, the hull of the galleon will be too large to fit through the neck of an ordinary bottle. To reduce the hull size, it must be sawed in two lengthwise along the line indicated on the plan. Do this in the early stages of construction before any rigging or detail work is done on the hull. Sand the two halves until they are smooth, and then rejoin them with short pins thrust through from the bottom. When the construction and painting of the vessel is complete, remove the pins and separate the two halves. Insert the lower section of the hull into the bottle and cement it in place on the putty sea. Next, insert the upper hull section and cement it in position on the lower. *After* the cement has hardened on both sections of the hull, raise the masts in the normal way and complete the work.

A second variation in technique is found in the installation of the mast shrouds. In this case the holes for shroudlines should be drilled completely through the hull rather than just through the rails. This permits a slightly greater spread to the shrouds because of the increased width of the hull at the lower level.